Copyright © 2022 Dani Haendiges.

All rights reserved. This book is protected by copyright. No part of this book may be reproduced or transmitted in any form or by any means, including as photocopies or scanned-in or other electronic copies, or utilized by any information storage and retrieval system without written permission from the copyright owner.

ISBN: 9781647045319

Printed in the United States of America.

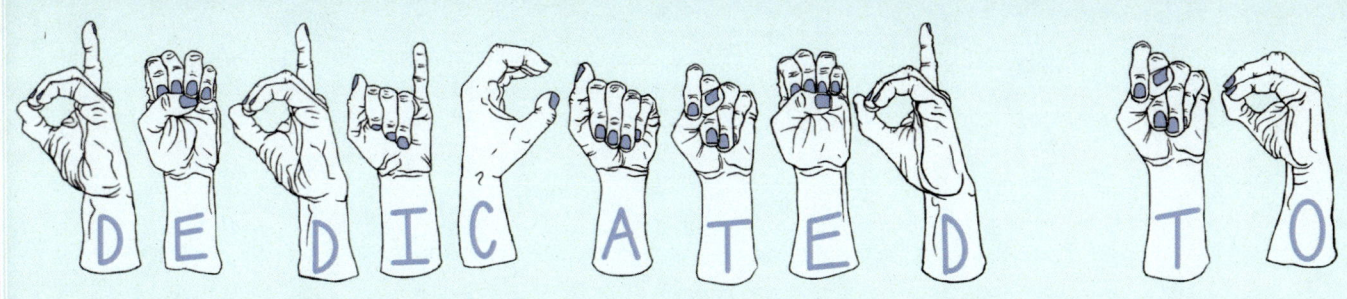

DEDICATED TO

My two wonderful kids, who, not only inspired this book, but also make me feel like I can do anything. I love you huge-big, to the moon and back!!

DWCD, for loving and supporting me every step of the way.

My parents, for believing in me for as long as I can remember; teaching me by example how to be the best mom I can be.

    and

Maria, for showing me how fiercely and unapologetically loving a person can be.

A is for apple, but only the green ones and only when they're sliced just right. That is the only way that Ollie will eat them. Ollie has **autism**, and he likes things just so. For Ollie, autism makes getting his words out difficult, and that can be frustrating. A is also for **ASL**, or **American Sign Language**, because communication is easier for him with his hands. ASL is used most in the deaf community, but it is also used by children who struggle with speech and are finding their voice through their hands!

I am Ollie's Mommy, and this story is about Ollie, a child who illustrates how helpful ASL can be for many people—hearing, deaf, and everything in between. One of the building blocks of ASL is finger spelling the ABCs. While most of the words illustrated in this book have individual signs, they will be shown finger spelled using the sign language alphabet in this book.

B is for bow. B is also for baby brother; Ollie is the baby of his family. His big sister, Rosie, is his biggest advocate, teacher, and helper. Rosie can use sign language too! Like Ollie, Rosie can hear just fine, but because of her baby brother, she has learned this skill to help her communicate with lots of different people. She loves to make new friends who might be different from herself; she has also befriended some deaf children who wouldn't otherwise be included. Her love for making everyone feel included and loving others for their differences makes me very proud.

B is for bulldozer. Sometimes Ollie is like a bulldozer. **Sensory processing** problems related to Ollie's autism make him seek hard pressure on his body. Sometimes, he doesn't realize how rough he is and accidentally hurts Rosie. Even though it upsets her, Rosie remembers that Ollie doesn't mean to slam things shut, break toys or play too rough with her: he is just a little different. Rosie is a very patient and empathetic big sister; she knows we all have different strengths and challenges! Having differences is one thing we all have in common.

B is for bow. Ollie's fine motor skills make some tasks tough, like holding a pencil correctly, using scissors, or tying a bow. Rosie loves to help her baby brother, so when he needs a hand to button his coat or tie his shoes, she is happy to help him.

C is for carrot, but only the long ones, never baby carrots. Ollie loves the crunch from carrots; it helps him feel his mouth and jaw. Due to Ollie's **sensory dysregulation,** he needs heavy physical input to feel balanced. He craves this pressure; to him, sensory input is like feeding a hunger. When he has these cravings for pressure on his jaw, and there is no sensory input available, he will often grind his teeth. We try hard to keep up with his sensory hunger before he feels the need to grind his teeth or engage in other potentially self-harming behavior.

C is for crash. Sometimes, Ollie feels like jumping to feel some impact on his feet or crashing onto the couch a few times to feel the weight of his body all at once. Just like we all need to eat to feel satisfied and be able to do other things, Ollie follows a "**sensory diet**" to keep himself feeling balanced throughout the day.

D is for daffodil. Daffodils are delicate. "Delicate" and "gentle" are hard concepts for Ollie, given his **sensory dysregulation**. Sometimes, all it takes is a squish from Mommy or a quick swing to help Ollie focus on keeping his hands gentle.

D is for development. Development is the process every person goes through as they learn and grow. When Ollie was very little, the term **"developmental milestones"** was used a lot by his doctors. But Mommy knew that development, like many other scales, is a wide spectrum. Just as we all see the world through a unique filter made up of all our experiences, so do we all develop and grow differently.

D is for different. We are all different, and that is one more way in which we are all the same.

E is for egg. Rosie and Ollie both love to help cook, and cracking the eggs is one of their favorite parts. It can be difficult for Rosie to hit the egg hard enough to crack the shell; Ollie hits them so hard that it's difficult to keep the shells out of the bowl! When they do get in, Ollie gets super focused on retrieving every last piece. To someone watching, it seems as if he is in his own world where nothing and no one else exists; only what he is focused on matters. Such hyper-focus is common with people who have autism: sometimes, it takes some extra time to start a new activity or finish something. We know it's important to offer that extra time to Ollie so he can feel successful in cooking too!

For Rosie, being Ollie's big sister can be challenging sometimes. Her emotions can be as fragile as an eggshell. When Ollie hurts Rosie's feelings, he tries his best to sign or say he is sorry. The hardest part for him can be making eye contact while he does it. For many people who are on the autism spectrum, eye contact can be hard—but it doesn't mean that they are not sincere. When Ollie signs that he's sorry, he means it. He loves Rosie; he just struggles sometimes to express it in a way she can easily understand.

F is for feather. Soft and delicate. Makes for a tickly touch. Ollie loves to have his back tickled, and gentle rubbing on his arms can be calming. Especially when you rub both arms at the same time in the same direction: this simultaneous touch on both arms triggers the two sides of our brains at the same time, which can help *everyone* calm down. You can try it yourself! Cross your arms and rub them from the shoulder to the elbows slowly while you take deep breaths. How do you feel afterward? Everyone can feel the effects of some of the techniques that Ollie uses to calm his senses down. We all need to balance our senses; some of us just need a reset more often than others do.

F is for force. The amount of force we use to perform different actions is controlled by our **proprioceptive sense**. You may have never heard of that sense because we are usually only taught about our five senses: hearing, sight, touch, taste, and smell. However, we all have many more senses that are less easily defined, such as proprioceptive, that are a big part of our lives whether we realize it or not. Sometimes, Ollie has a tough time judging how hard he closes doors or sets down cups and toys. It may seem as though he is slamming cabinets or throwing his glass down, but he really just has difficulty regulating how much force his hands are using. When his proprioceptive sense needs some input, he might stomp his feet or bang his head on things to feel his own weight and force in space. Sometimes feathers, sometimes furious force—for Ollie, it is all about balancing.

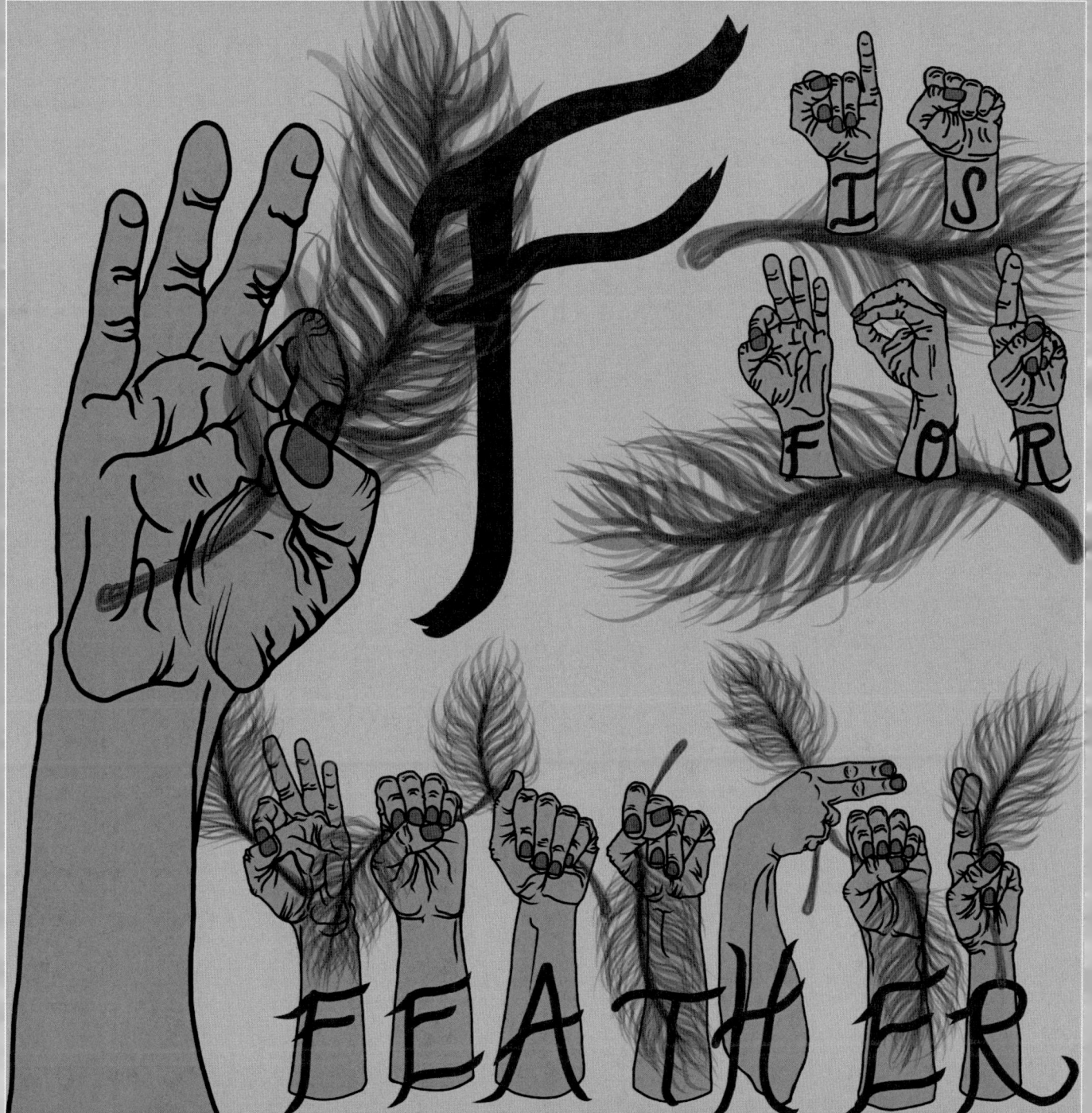

G is for glasses. Many of our friends wear glasses to see better. Their eyes need help to see the world clearly. Your eyes are the tool to take in the colors and shapes that you see. That information is then sent to your brain to be organized and explained. For most people, this process happens without them even realizing it. You may think you just see a house or a car with your eyes, but really, you see colors and shapes with your eyes and then your brain interprets those shapes as objects you know. For people with sensory processing problems, and often autism, the images and lights received as input by their eyes are too much for their brains to process all at once. For Ollie, this can mean that blinking lights or things that spin can fill up all his brain space, leaving no room for other thoughts to enter. He might look like he has a blank stare, but he is actually just taking in all that information at his own pace. Just like how people who wear glasses need help (glasses) for the visual tool (eyes) to see well, Ollie needs help for his brain to organize and make sense of the visual information. His eyes work just fine taking in the shapes and colors; the extra time he needs is to understand them.

H is for hummingbird. A hummingbird needs to refuel about seven times per hour while they are awake. Holy cow! Can you imagine needing a meal every 8.5 minutes? That makes eating an almost constant job for them. Just as a hummingbird must satisfy their hunger amid a very busy schedule, Ollie needs to have his "sensory diet," where he engages in sensory activities regularly throughout the day. A sensory diet and a strict schedule are essential for Ollie; he functions best when his days are broken down into tiny increments and he knows what's coming next. We include times to have sensory breaks and try to ensure that everything happens at the same time and in the same order. Ollie feels the most balanced and in control when he has consistency in his activities.

I is for Ivy. Like so many things in the life of a person with special needs or even a parent of that person, things seem to grow and compound on themselves until the main idea is lost entirely—like a house that gets lost in the ivy that envelopes it. In Ollie's life, this has forced our family to lose sight of ideas that might otherwise be important to a child his age. In some ways, I use this idea to focus on the bigger battles we are fighting and let the little things go. For example, he may be potty training late, but we are working really hard on talking and that is more important right now. On the other hand, sometimes Ollie's autism can make it difficult to remember that he needs to learn the same lessons as any other child his age; they may just need to be taught in a different way or he may need to be encouraged in creative ways. Like *sharing*: sharing is really hard, but Ollie still has to learn how to do it. His autism cannot be an excuse for poor behavior; he simply needs a different approach to teaching him what is right and wrong.

I is for Intelligent. Ollie is very intelligent. His ability to express himself is limited, but we need to remember not to treat him like a baby. We all have different strengths and weaknesses; our being unique is something we all have in common. For Ollie, understanding numbers and math comes very naturally. What are some things you are really good at? He finds making eye contact very challenging. What is something that is hard for you?

J is for Juice. I will never forget Ollie's first real communication beyond one-word or single sign responses. He was sitting on the kitchen counter making sounds we knew to mean he wanted something. Daddy and I asked with our voices and hands what he wanted. Suddenly he reached for a coffee mug, presented, and signed the words, "apple," "juice," and "want" and said "cup." Those few words spoken with his little hands and tiny voice carried a meaning that was so much more than the sum of its parts. I was an expression of his needs that would have previously been whining and frustration at his inability to be understood.

These small moments are monumental to parents of neurodiverse kids, and many parents of neurotypical children cannot understand their weight or the struggles that preceded them. It can be very isolating for neurodiverse kids and their caretakers. The best thing we can do is try to empathize and relate; to be inclusive and supportive.

J is for jokes. For some **neurodiverse** people, humor and sarcasm don't make sense. For many, everything they say is completely literal. They speak only their truth, and it may not be as gentle or socially acceptable as how other people would say it. Ollie might say that a dish tastes "too yucky," while most people learn to be more polite when someone makes them food to eat. Ollie does not mean to hurt the cook's feelings; he just has a hard time understanding how to speak gently when someone's feelings might get hurt. For some people on the autism spectrum, the idea that the "truth" they are saying could be something unkind is confusing. They also may struggle with non-verbal cues; they may not understand the facial expressions that to others are very apparent. Patience is so important in accepting others exactly as they are; we all need patience and care, and we should take care of others in the same way.

K is for Kaleidoscope. A kaleidoscope is a series of mirrors that distorts the light and images we see into beautiful patterns that can move and change as you turn it and look around. These patterns can be very pleasing and calming to our brains. For Ollie, patterns are very soothing, because his mind tends to work very logically and in a certain order. Sometimes, when our brains are tired, something like a kaleidoscope can be overstimulating and overwhelming since it makes our visual senses work hard to process what we are looking at. In this way, for someone with a **sensory processing** issue, seeing bright colors or busy patterns that can otherwise be relaxing, can also be too much to handle. For Ollie, this is never so obvious as it is with a car wash. Sometimes Ollie will ask to go through the car wash because the sounds and lights serve his senses; other times Mom will try to go through the car wash to help calm an agitated little guy but it will do quite the opposite. When the brain space that can be tickled by the car wash is taken over by something that is upsetting to him, adding more information to the mix can be devastating to the sensory balance.

L is for Lollipop. Ollie has a toxic romance with sugar. While sugar is something that he will rarely turn down, the crash afterward is very hard for his little body to manage and even harder to explain to him. He is sent into a downward spiral that leaves him feeling out of control and imbalanced, which causes destructive behavior. Because of this, sweets are only rare treats and have to be timed just right. Just the same, Ollie loves the treat of a lollipop! What is your favorite treat?

L is for listening. Listening skills are very important, being able to actively listen to one another—not just hear each other's words while waiting to respond, but really taking the time and effort to soak in what they are trying to say. As family, friends, and teachers of neurodiverse people, we need to use a special set of listening skills to make sure that we understand the real meaning of what is being said, both with words and non-verbal cues. Many of our friends with communication challenges use different ways to make their needs known. As their advocates and friends, we can do our best to be patient and try to take in the whole picture of what is being expressed.

L is for listening. Listening to instructions or even responding to his own name when Ollie is deeply focused on something else is nearly impossible. Sometimes, just repeating or rephrasing the question makes it possible to grab his attention and help him to answer or perform the task. At other times, using a physical cue (a tap on the shoulder, a hand on his back) can help break his concentration on his other focus and get him to respond. But sometimes, no amount of repetition will get his attention, and it's as if he can't hear you at all; some of those times, a physical cue will upset him because having his whole brain focused on whatever it is, is very important to him. I think it is important to remember that when our friends like Ollie have a hard time listening, we must be as patient as we can but remain calm and persistent in our efforts to help them understand what we are trying to convey. It may take time and some creativity to make a connection to our friends and help them listen, but in the end, these connections are very worthwhile. All people are different, and we all learn and communicate a little differently, but that is one thing we all have in common!

M is for mandolin. The mandolin is a challenging instrument to learn and even harder to master. The sounds that can be made with it are beautiful, but having to learn the different shapes your hands need to form can make learning to play the Mandolin, or any instrument, very frustrating. It takes lots and lots of practice. People who have a talent for music still have to work hard to get their hands to learn the motions that are needed to make music on instruments. For Ollie, some things that seem simpler to us may take just as much practice and work as learning to play the mandolin. To keep his right foot on a bicycle pedal or to hold a fork correctly can be very frustrating for him and take lots of focus.

M is for music. Music is very important for well-being. Music can set the mood or express a new one. A steady rhythm can be a great way to re-center and help focus for Ollie; the music can have an almost mesmerizing effect. He loves songs that have a strong beat; they are settling for him and help him focus his mind and body.

M is for mindfulness. Music and Meditative practice help make us all a little more mindful. Rosie is excellent at helping her brother find a sensory balance through deep breaths and practicing mindfulness. Do you know how to practice mindfulness? Can you sit and quietly just feel your breath go in and out? That is a way to practice mindfulness!

M is for math. Ollie loves numbers. He counts when he gets overwhelmed, then he often starts doing addition problems out loud. This repetitive math serves to help Ollie make sense of his situation; he uses something familiar to him to calm his brain down so it can take in the new information. Do you have a saying or song that you use to feel better?

N is for neurodiversity. **Neurodiversity** is a very important term. Ollie has autism and struggles with sensory input; he is considered **Neurodiverse**. Rosie only worries about sensory dysregulation as it relates to her brother; she doesn't struggle to balance her sensory input. Rosie is considered **Neurotypical**. Similar to the way autism is on a spectrum, the level of variation a person has with learning, interacting with others, and focusing and managing their moods forms the spectrum of neurodiversity. A person can be considered neurodiverse because they are dyslexic or have an attention disorder. This term has addressed a controversial topic that a person with autism cannot be separated from their autism. It cannot be cured—that is not the goal! Ollie's brain is special and unique. He learns differently from many other children, but he still learns. He interacts with his friends in a different way than many other children, but he still loves to play with his friends! Just like you, Ollie is special and unique in lots of ways!

O is for Octopus. An octopus has hundreds of suction cups on each of its eight tentacles. Did you know that they can control each one independently? Just like you can move each of your arms, legs, and fingers separately, an octopus can use each suction cup by itself. Have you ever tried to learn a new skill, like riding a bike or tying your shoes, and felt like your feet or fingers just won't do what you want them to? It feels as though you need more brain space to manage each part. For some people, just managing their limbs can feel like they have hundreds of octopus suckers that they are trying to move at once in different directions. For some people like Ollie, learning to get one hand to communicate with the other or making their feet work in a pattern is a bigger challenge to conquer than you might realize. We need to be kind and patient with our friends who may need some extra help getting their bearings or managing their limbs. When we celebrate our differences and help others do better, we all do a little bit better!

P is for peacock. Peacocks use their big, bright feathers to attract friends and also to look bigger when they are threatened by another animal. Their feathers serve two purposes, by doing the same thing! Sometimes, the beautiful colors are meant to attract attention, and at other times, they are supposed to be intimidating. We all have ways to make ourselves look different. We wear different clothes to go to different places. We wear sunglasses to keep the sun out of our eyes, but also for fashion. Our clothing and accessories are like peacock feathers serving many purposes. Ollie has some special clothes too! Ollie wears special shirts sometimes that hold a tracker. Ollie can get very distracted and wander away. I worry that he will get lost! His special shirts give him a super tight hug to help him feel regulated, but they are also specially made to hold his tracking machine. For some people with autism and other differences, getting lost or wandering away is a big concern; these devices are very helpful in keeping them safe. Have you ever gotten distracted in a store and looked up for your parent, and they weren't right there? It's a scary feeling. This machine helps us prevent those scary situations.

Q is for question. So many questions. As parents, we have questions about what certain diagnoses mean for our children. How can we better help our children? What should we do? How "atypical" will our child be? The question many people used to ask was, "How can we make our children more like other children?" but really, we need to ask, "How can we change the world to accommodate these people and their differences?" Every day, I think about what I can do to help Ollie feel balanced and successful, and the more I focus on working around his need to line things up perfectly, or take extra time finishing tasks, the more I help our world suit him just the way he is. We may ask, "Will they get better? Will they grow out of this?" but it is important to know that our neurodiverse kids are not sick; they are just wired differently. Their brains work differently from most, but not incorrectly. We need to help them learn and grow, but also understand that their sensory needs and other quirky behaviors are not necessarily things to be changed so much as accommodated.

Q is for questions. Ollie asks lots of questions over and over again. "Why?", "What's that?" Ollie's need to understand the world around him is just as intense and curious as any other child. Sometimes in conversations, Ollie will just insert questions such as, "What's your name?" He tends to use the same questions over and over. "What's your name?" is a favorite because he knows the other person's response before they say it and even their follow up question. He can assume they will ask his name next and that is another question he knows how to answer without much thought needed. This scripting of conversations is common among neurodiverse people because it can take some of the anxiety and confusion out of talking to others; an otherwise daunting task. Scripting so he can have conversation helps Ollie feel included.

R is for Repeat. R is for Recite. R is for Repeat. When you are talking to someone, do you ever respond to a question without really thinking about what was asked? Someone may ask how you are, and you say "fine" before really asking yourself how you feel. Other times, the automatic response doesn't work; you really have to consider what is being asked before you can give an answer. Ollie will often recite what seems like a script. While he knows that he is supposed to respond at that point in the conversation, and he understands that there is a back-and-forth component to social interaction, he may not be able to register the question in what he has been taught is the right time frame. Because of this, he may just repeat the words said to him before answering the question or responding. This is referred to as **echolalia**, the repetition of words whose meaning one may or may not understand. As with humor, non-verbal cues and facial expressions can be challenging for neurodiverse people. Ollie is working hard to understand how conversation works.

R is for Repeat. To get through our day, I need to present the next three steps on our visual schedule constantly. There is a very repetitive component to making it work. Ollie needs a 10-, 5-, 2-, and 1-minute warning before each step, as well as a reminder of the two steps that will follow. I often repeat each step five times or more, working to get and keep his attention, and then get him to agree to the plan. Ollie doesn't always want to do what he needs to, and I never want to force him to do things. Ollie is an independent person with his own opinions that need to be respected. He does the right thing most of the time and just needs some extra warnings and planning to feel in control of his life.

S is for Superhero. I knew a superhero. Her name was Maria. Maria had a brother who had not only autism but also trisomy 21, better known as Down Syndrome. This combination was even recently thought to be impossible, but beating the odds runs strong in this family. Maria, like Rosie, grew up feeling it was her duty to protect her brother. She did this valiantly. My favorite story she ever told me about this, is the zoo story. One day when Maria was nine or ten years old, she and her brother went on a trip to the zoo with a babysitter. They were playing on the playground at the zoo when her little brother climbed to the top of the slide and sat contemplating his next step. When the little boy who was next in line on the ladder to go down the slide felt he had been waiting too long and got no real response from the little brother, he gently went around him to go down the slide. Little did he know that Maria had been watching from a nearby spot to make sure no one bothered her brother while he figured out what his next step was. As Maria approached the boy to thank him for being kind and just going around her little brother, the boy's mom intercepted him. With Maria very close by, the mother said, "Well I'm glad you went around him. I don't want you to catch whatever he has." Maria promptly told this woman that nothing was wrong with or contagious about her little brother and smacked that mom in the face. Soon after the interaction came about, a proud Maria, her unknowing little brother, and their terribly flustered babysitter were escorted out of the zoo by security.

While neither I nor Maria's parents condone violence as a solution, we admire her fiercely protective spirit. Maria was as fiercely loving, advocating, and encouraging on that day as she was when I met her many years later (there had been no further physical altercations). I see in Rosie that same fire to keep her brother safe. We can all be superheroes for people who have special needs. We can simply be open to understanding other people's challenges; we can inform others about how our different ways of interacting with the world are what we all have in common.

T is for Tyrannosaurus Rex. Ollie loves dinosaurs. He has a set of fifty magnets with different depictions of dinosaurs on them. One day, while looking at the cluster of these magnets on the door, he looked at me and said, "Oh no! Parasaurolophus! Missing! Where he go?"

This is unbelievable for so many reasons. For Ollie, this is a very advanced statement simply for the complexity of the sentences, but the truly amazing part was that he pronounced the name of a dinosaur—that I didn't realize existed—perfectly! It was absolutely unbelievable! This little boy who cannot pronounce his own name can say "Parasaurolophus" with perfect diction.

The next thing one might note as unusual is his ability to look at a group of forty-nine magnets and recognize instantaneously that one (not to mention which one) was missing. For some children with autism, the tendency to have laser focus on things that we may see as irrelevant or strange can serve to hone specific, unusual skills. For Ollie, when a subject is of interest to him, he has the ability to use all the power of his brain to focus on only that, whereas for most of us, there is always "background noise"—what we are doing later, what happened yesterday, homework, family, etc. Ollie has tunnel vision focusing all his brain cells on one single thing.

T is for time. Parents often complain about the amount of time it takes to get ready with kids. With a child who has autism, this time frame is increased exponentially. Every shirt has the potential to feel scratchy and send Ollie into a meltdown. A sock seam misaligned with his toes is a recipe for having to start your morning from scratch. These may seem like overreactions, but we must remember that what may feel like a scratchy tag to us can feel equivalent to a bed of nails to Ollie.

U is for Unicorn. A unicorn is a mythical creature. It can represent an unattainable goal or a set of impossible standards never to be reached. The idea of what is "normal" can be represented by the unicorn. All of us fall somewhere on a spectrum. No one is 100% anything! Just one more thing we all have in common is our being perfectly imperfect. The best we can be will never meet all the idealistic standards that exist, and that's okay! We are all very different in our strengths and our challenges, and we all fall on a multitude of levels on an infinite number of bell curves.

U is for Unicorn. Rosie loves unicorns. She is the other reason for this illustration representing a unicorn. She can sometimes feel left out because so much of our time and effort go into helping her brother feel comfortable and successful in his life. Rosie is so very smart and capable: she doesn't require as much planning and input to get through her days, and sometimes, she yearns to get offered the help that he gets. While Ollie's sensory dysregulation is marked on documents as a disability, to Rosie, it is something she may feel envious of, just for the attention he gets. So, this illustration is for her.

V is for volume. The volume of sounds is crucial to Ollie's experiences. A seemingly reasonable sound to most people can be grating to a person with sensory processing issues. For Ollie, this means that an alarm going off is incapacitating. The sound of music in the car may require noise-canceling headphones to be enjoyable, or he may hum the tones made by the tires on the road with perfect pitch to calm himself.

V is for video. I very regularly use a "first, then" system to help keep Ollie on task and help motivate him to do things that he may not be interested in doing. Changes in the routine or even just going from one task to a less preferred one can be very challenging. Even with adequate advanced notice, he often needs incentive to get dressed or brush his teeth. For him, watching a video is the best reward.

V is for vestibular. The **vestibular sense** is one of the many senses we have that are often overlooked once the first five are taught to us as children. Your vestibular sense is how you process your balance using the inner ear. If you start to fall, the sense that processes the feeling is your vestibular sense. People like Ollie often need vestibular input to feel balanced; swinging or rocking can help him reset his senses.

V is for visual schedule. Ollie bases each day on a visual schedule—small pictures of every step in his day that help make our plans visual instead of a written list, so that he can better imagine his day. Routine is very important to Ollie; it helps him feel a sense of control in his world. Do you have a routine you like to do every day?

W is for Watch. I never wore a watch. Punctuality was never my strength, but while all children thrive on consistency and routine, this is magnified a ton in the case of some children with autism. I have two dozen alarms on my phone to remind me when it's time to set the table for dinner, and then another when we need to eat. There is an alarm that tells us when it's time to leave, but also three to give warnings about when we brush our teeth, get dressed, and put on our shoes. Keeping time is crucial for the first time in my life, because to Ollie, staying on a routine is a very strict process. For many children with autism and sensory issues, meltdowns can be avoided by staying on schedule down to the very last detail. Are there things in your life that you expect to happen at a certain time? Would you feel confused and maybe off-balance if they were suddenly changed? For Ollie, adding a stop for gas on the way to an event when it wasn't explained in the original plan is crushing. It is the equivalent of driving home with your family and finding that your house is not there. We need to work hard to make very detailed plans so that Ollie knows what is going to happen and can handle the transitions.

X is for Checklist.

Yes, I know the word "checklist" does not start with the letter "X"—but "x-ing" items off a list is crucial. Life with Ollie is constantly revolving around a checklist. Our visual schedule is made up of illustrated magnets that hang on the door. It puts Ollie and Rosie in control of completing tasks and checking them off the list, as well as knowing what is coming next in our day. While there are still many warnings and timers with alarms, knowing the basic steps of the day and having the ability to put check-mark magnets on top of each event/task gives Rosie and Ollie the control over removing the task from the list.

i s f o r

c h e c k -

l i s t

Y is for Yin and Yang. The Yin Yang concept is all about balance—a balance of different qualities that are natural in humanity. It was once explained to me that in every good there is a little bit of bad, and in every bad, there is a little bit of good. While an event may seem devastating, there is always a bright spot.

No parent goes into childbirth expecting a neurodiverse child. No parent assumes that their child will be developmentally delayed, but sometimes, it happens. These very unique children are born every day. While it is scary realizing that your style of parenting is going to need to be different from what you expected, so much good can come from it. Ollie has ignited a passion and drive in me as a parent, a person, a mother, and an artist. His atypical brain and developmental journey that once blindsided me has made me hungry to learn about his different abilities and mold our family's routine to be as conducive as possible to his success. In essence, discovering that Ollie is different was at first scary and seemed like a roadblock, but this perceived speed bump was really a launchpad. Yes, we will do the work and learn to adapt to Ollie's way of learning. We should all learn to say "yes" to changing the world to make space for neurodiverse people, not molding the neurodiverse to fit in our structure. To be neurodiverse is not a negative thing, it should just be one more difference between people—and having differences is one thing we all have in common.

Z is for Zig-Zag. The road to helping Ollie achieve what he has so far and facilitating his growth and feeling successful in life has been a long one, and often not a straight line. Many times, it seemed we took one step forward only to take two steps back. Ollie needed an advocate just to be evaluated because his doctor didn't feel that he was delayed in his development enough for it to be a priority. There have been countless hours spent making plans to help transition smoothly from one activity to the next; weeks of journals written, documenting the progress (or lack thereof) from the new system, only to find out that it was not effective for him. Every time we achieve a goal, it seems that there is a new challenge to overcome. Everyone is different. We all have our own strengths and weaknesses that lead our journey. None of those journeys are walked in a straight line. It's just important that we embrace our own zig-zag—our own growth and development chart—and keep trying to do better. Respect others and accept them for who they are. Even when it's hard, we just need to keep working on it. Kids don't always get it right the first time, and neither do parents. Mom and Dad can't always circumvent the meltdowns; we just keep striving to do our best. Let's all keep doing our best to keep everyone included: we are a part of the same perfectly imperfect, all-over-all-the-spectrums team.

Made in the USA
Monee, IL
05 November 2022